Preparatory

Mid-Elementary

A DOZEN A DAY SONGBOOK

Includes Online Audio!

Each piece includes two audio tracks: one with piano and orchestration at a practice tempo, and one with just the orchestration at a faster performance tempo. With our exclusive ***Playback+*** feature, you can change the tempo even more without altering the pitch, plus set loop points for continuous repetition of tricky measures.

To access audio, visit:
www.halleonard.com/mylibrary

Enter Code
3662-1812-4185-2964

Book
ISBN 978-1-4234-7559-0

Book/Audio
ISBN 978-1-4234-7562-0

EXCLUSIVELY DISTRIBUTED BY

HAL•LEONARD®
CORPORATION
7777 W. BLUEMOUND RD. P.O. BOX 13819
MILWAUKEE, WISCONSIN 53213

Visit Hal Leonard Online at
www.halleonard.com

NOTE TO TEACHERS

This collection of Broadway, movie and pop hits can be used on its own or as supplementary material to the iconic *A Dozen A Day* technique series by Edna Mae Burnam. The pieces have been arranged to progress gradually, applying concepts and patterns from Burnam's technical exercises whenever possible. Teacher accompaniments and suggested guidelines for use with the original series are also provided.

These arrangements are excellent supplements for any method and may also be used for sight-reading practice for more advanced students.

CONTENTS

Heart and Soul

from the Paramount Short Subject A SONG IS BORN

Use with A Dozen A Day Preparatory Book, after Group I (page 9).

Words by Frank Loesser
Music by Hoagy Carmichael
Arranged by Carolyn Miller

With a lilt (♩♩ = ♩♪ triplet)

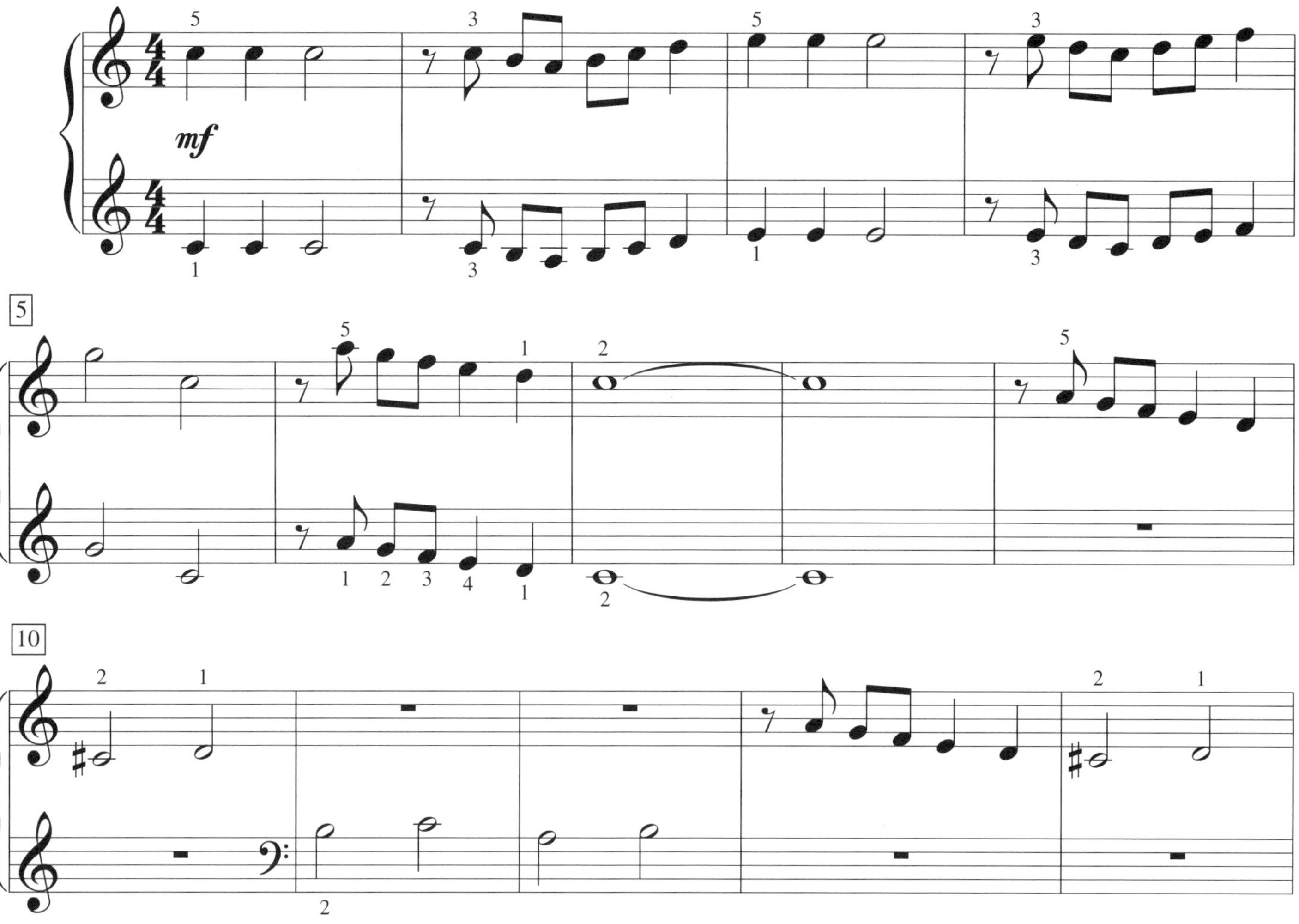

Accompaniment (Student plays one octave higher than written.)

With a lilt (♩♩ = ♩♪ triplet)

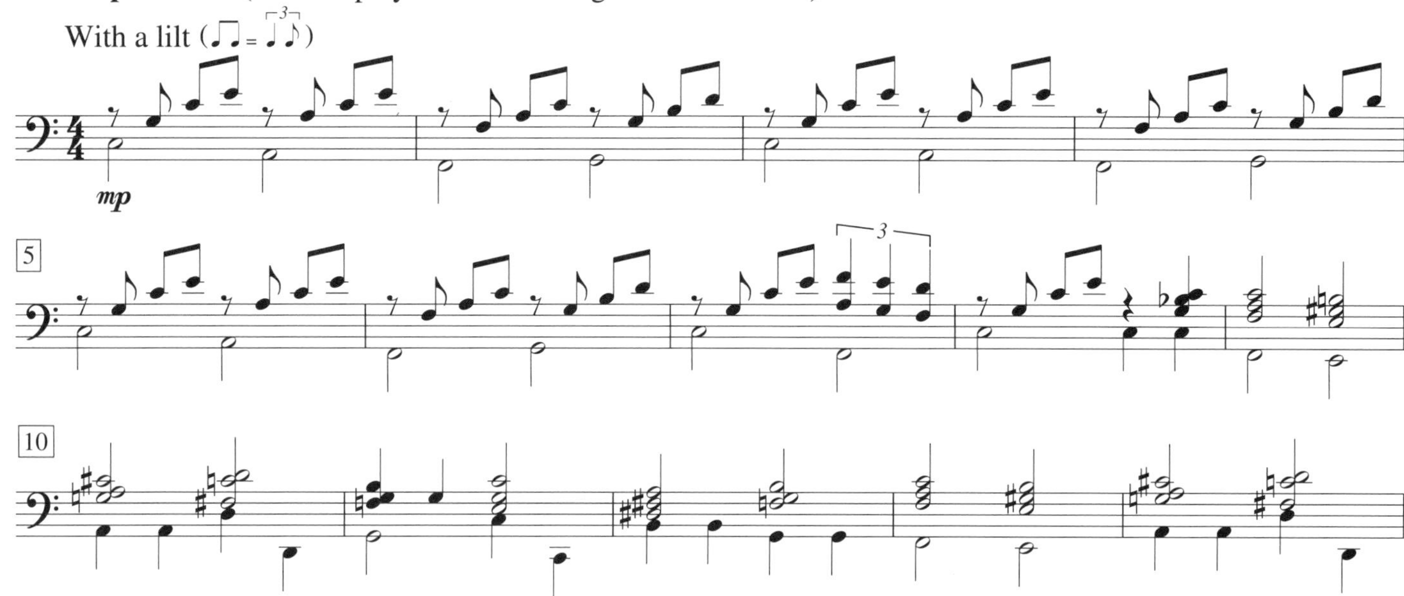

15
2
f
2
19
5
3
1
5
23
2
4
1
2
1
L.H. over
2
3
5
15
mf
19
23

Little April Shower

from Walt Disney's BAMBI

Use after Group I (page 9).

Words by Larry Morey
Music by Frank Churchill
Arranged by Carolyn Miller

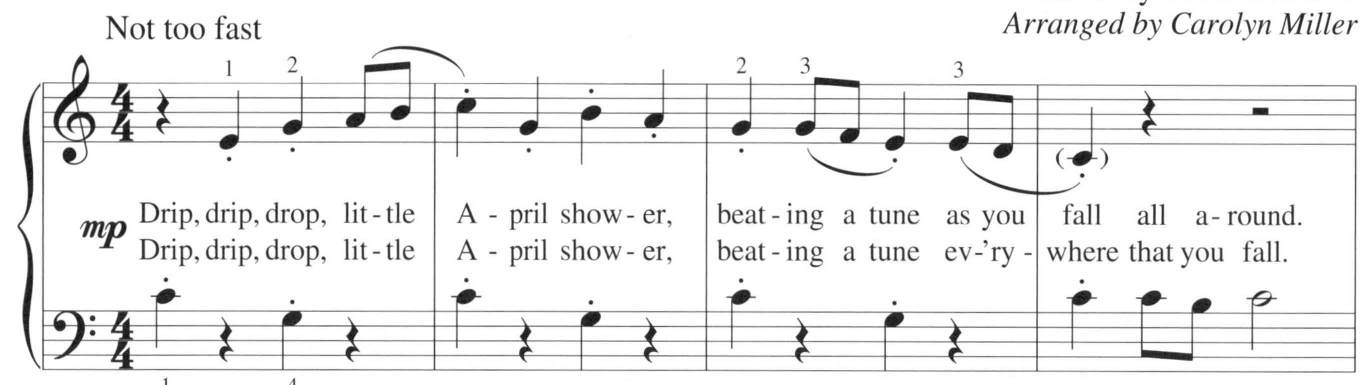

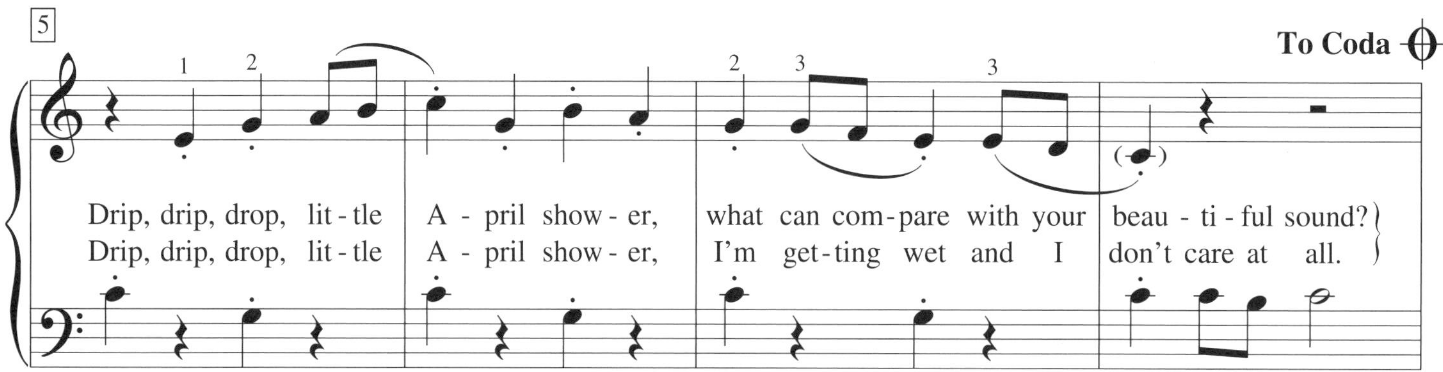

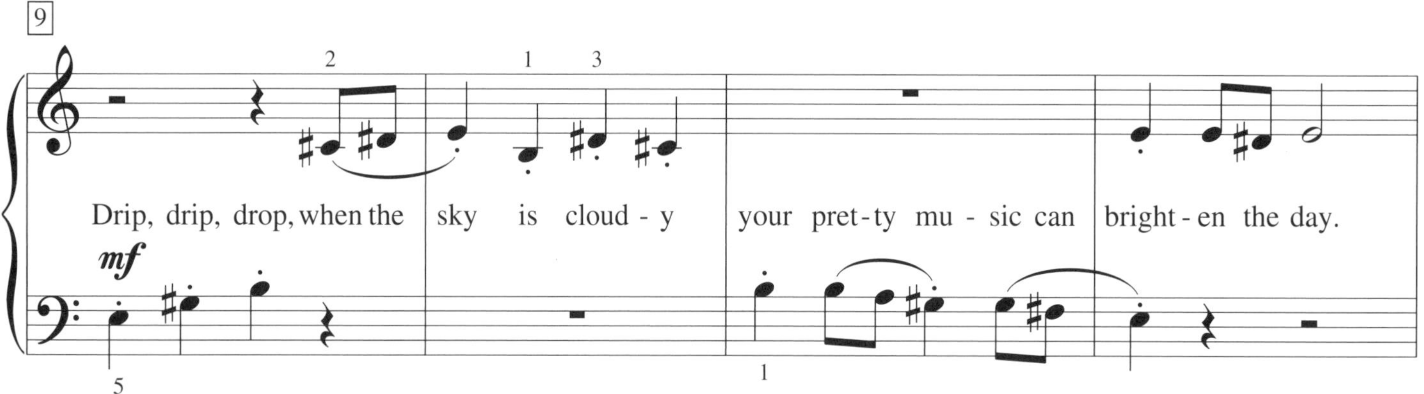

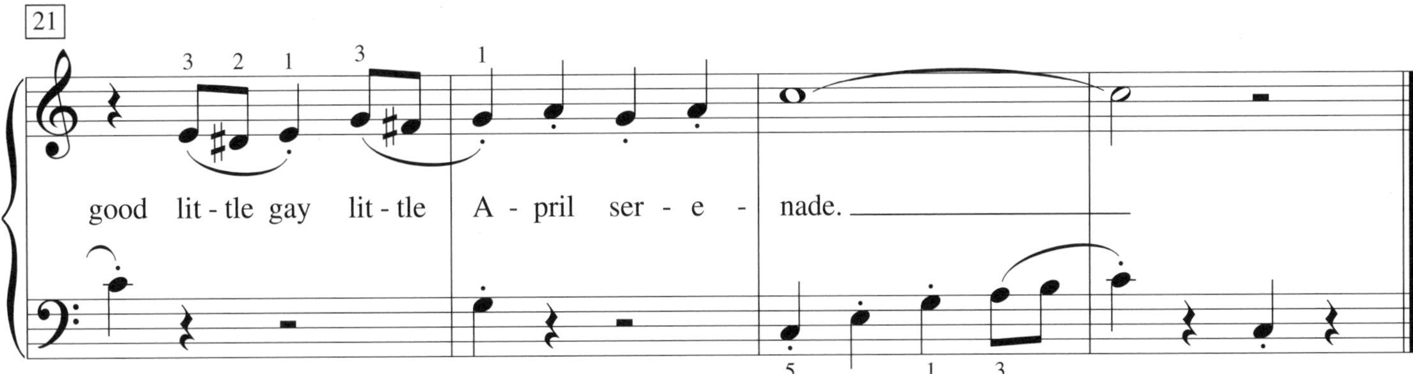

* **D.C. al Coda** means return to the beginning of the piece, play to the **To Coda** indication, then skip to the measure marked **CODA** to finish the piece.

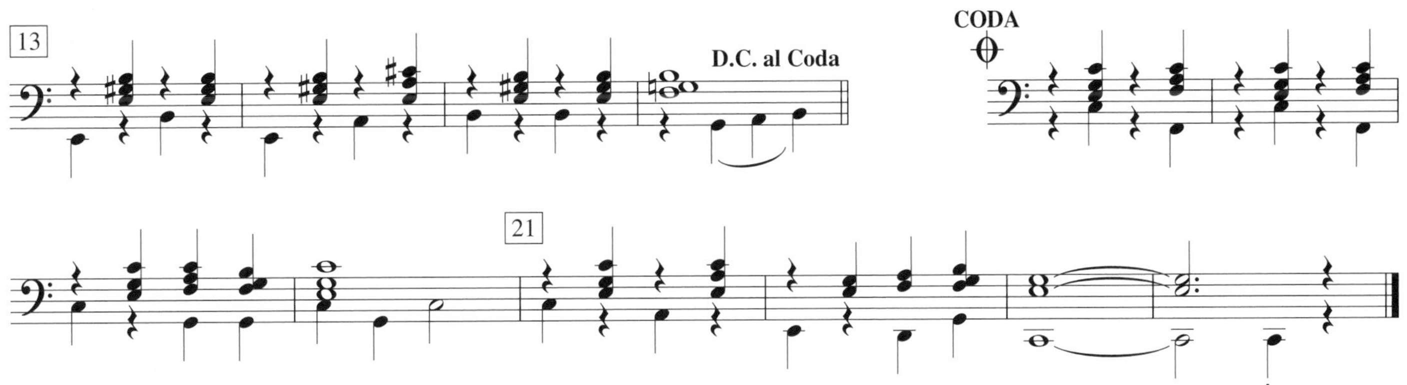

The Way You Look Tonight

from SWING TIME

Use after Group II (page 13).

Words by Dorothy Fields
Music by Jerome Kern
Arranged by Carolyn Miller

At a relaxed tempo

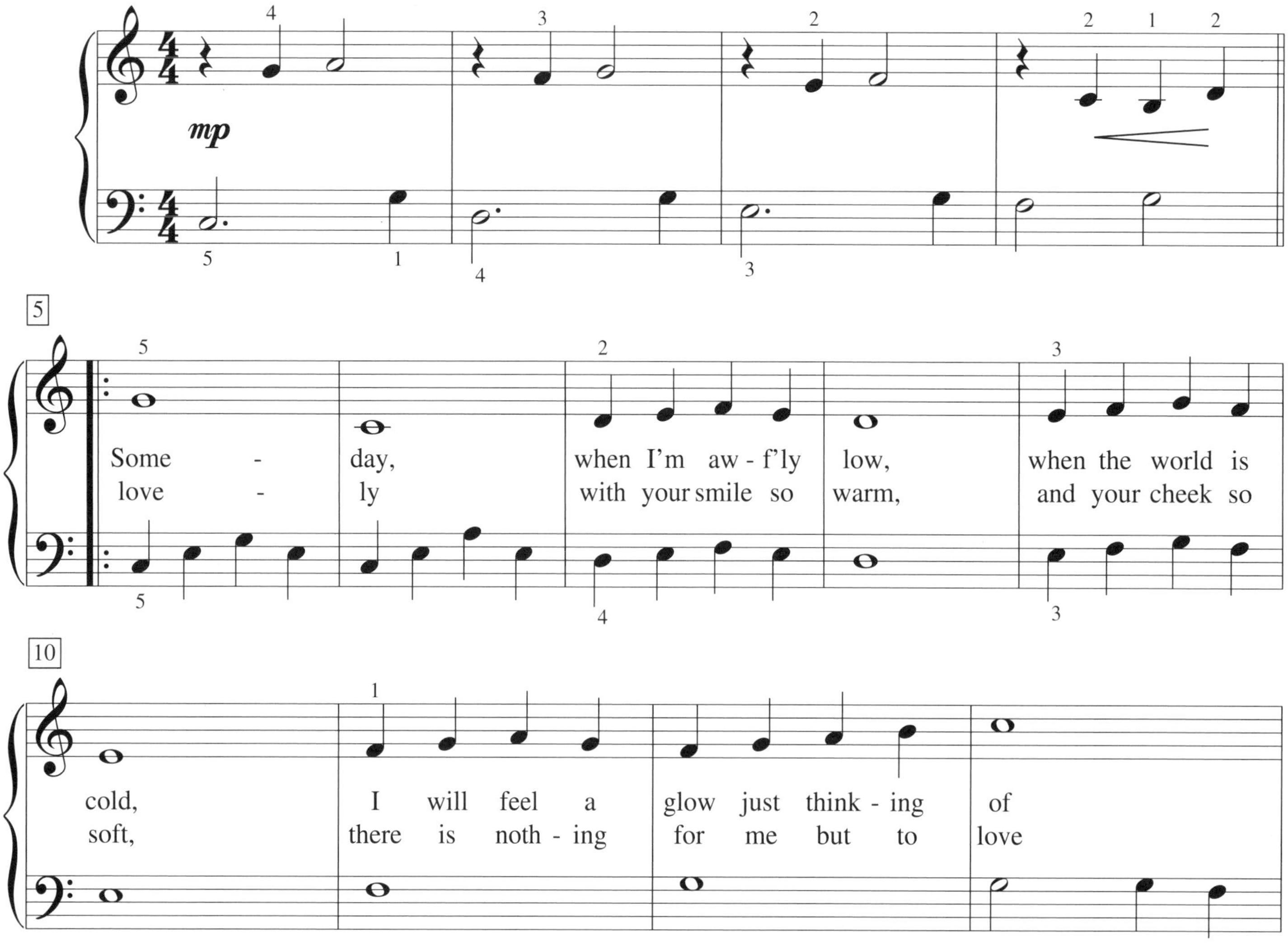
mp
5
Some - day, when I'm aw - f'ly low, when the world is
love - ly with your smile so warm, and your cheek so
10
cold, I will feel a glow just think - ing of
soft, there is noth - ing for me but to love

Accompaniment (Student plays one octave higher than written.)

At a relaxed tempo

mp
5
p
10

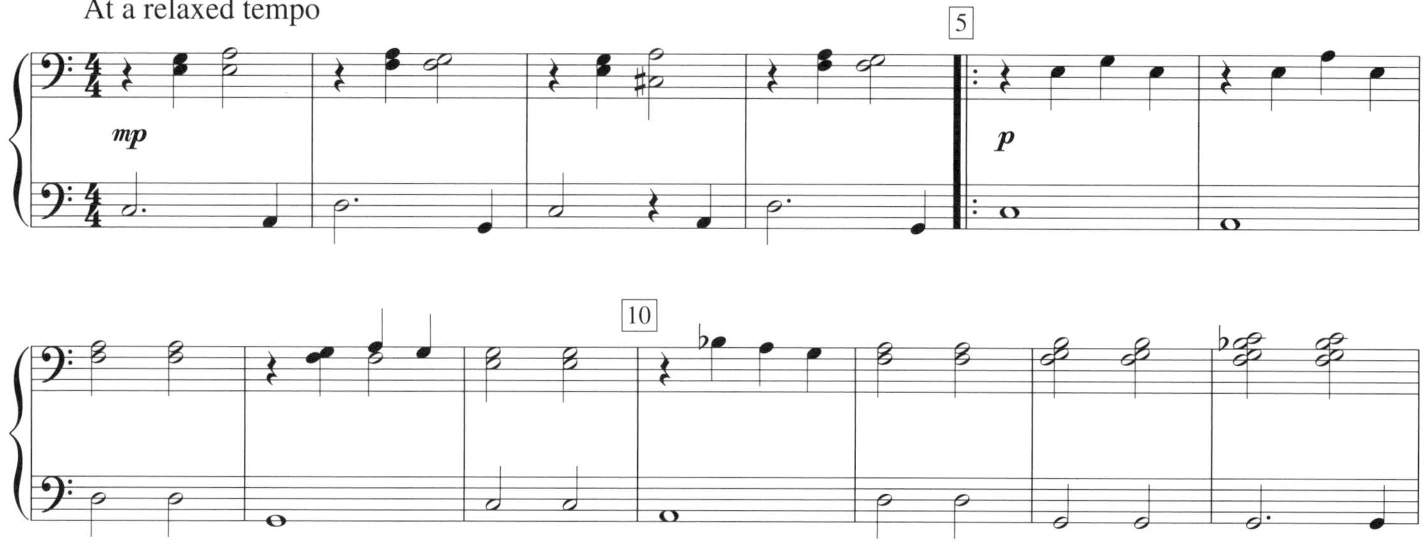

14
1
3 4
5
you
and the way you
look to - night.
you
just the way you
look to - night.
18
1.
2.
2 3
4
2 3
2 1
5
Oh, but you're
22
3
2
Just the way you
look to - night.
p
2
14
18
1.
2.
22
pp
8vb

Yellow Submarine

Use after Group II (page 13).

Words and Music by John Lennon
and Paul McCartney
Arranged by Carolyn Miller

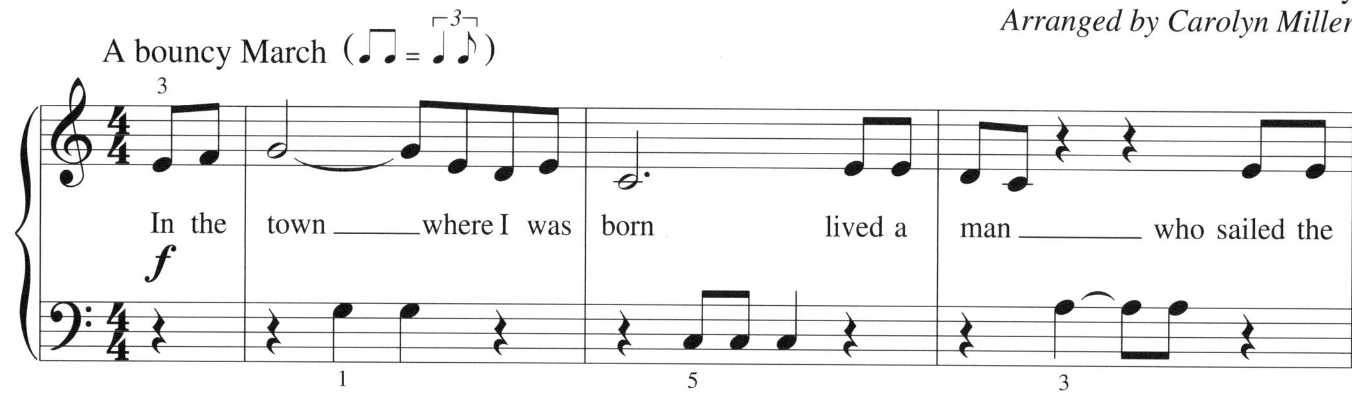

Accompaniment (Student plays one octave higher than written.)

13
lived ___ be-neath the waves in our yel - low sub-ma - rine.
17
We all live in a yel-low sub-ma-rine, yel-low sub-ma-rine, yel-low sub-ma-rine.
21
We all live in a yel-low sub-ma-rine, yel-low sub-ma-rine, yel-low sub-ma-rine.
25
13
17
21
25

Part of Your World

from Walt Disney's THE LITTLE MERMAID

Use after Group III (page 18).

Music by Alan Menken
Lyrics by Howard Ashman
Arranged by Carolyn Miller

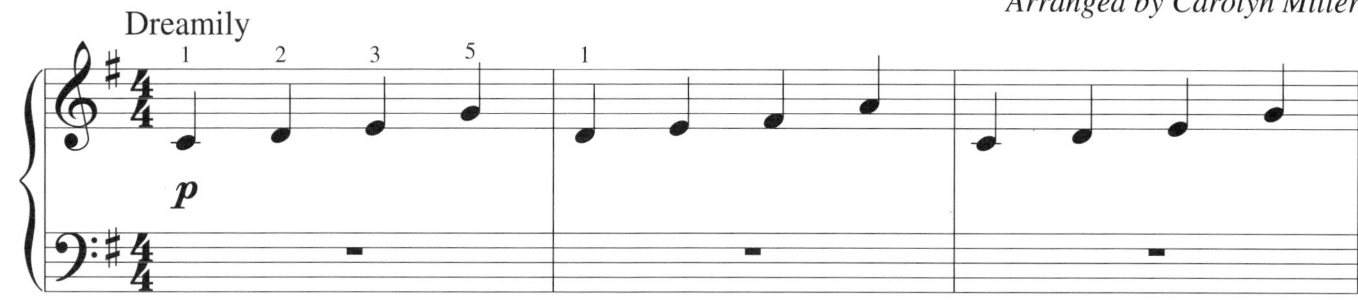

Accompaniment (Student plays one octave higher than written.)

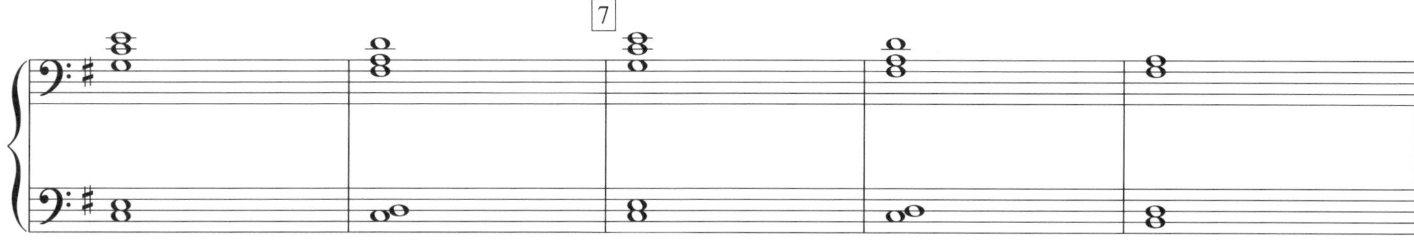

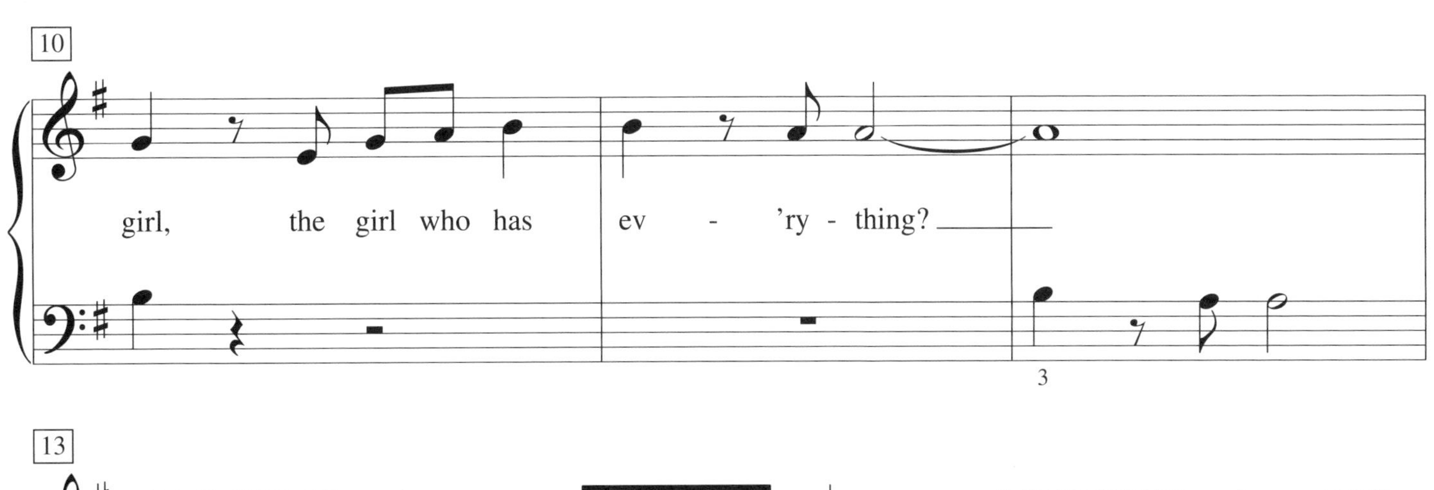
10
girl, the girl who has ev - ’ry - thing?
3

13
Look at this trove, treas-ures un - told. How man - y won - ders can

16
3
one cav - ern hold? Look-ing a - round here you’d think, “Sure, she’s got

10
13

16

19
ev - 'ry - thing." I've got gad - gets and giz - mos a -
22
plen - ty. I've got who - zits and what - zits ga - lore. You want
25
thing-a - ma - bobs? I've got twen - ty. But who cares? No big
rit.
19
22
25
rit.

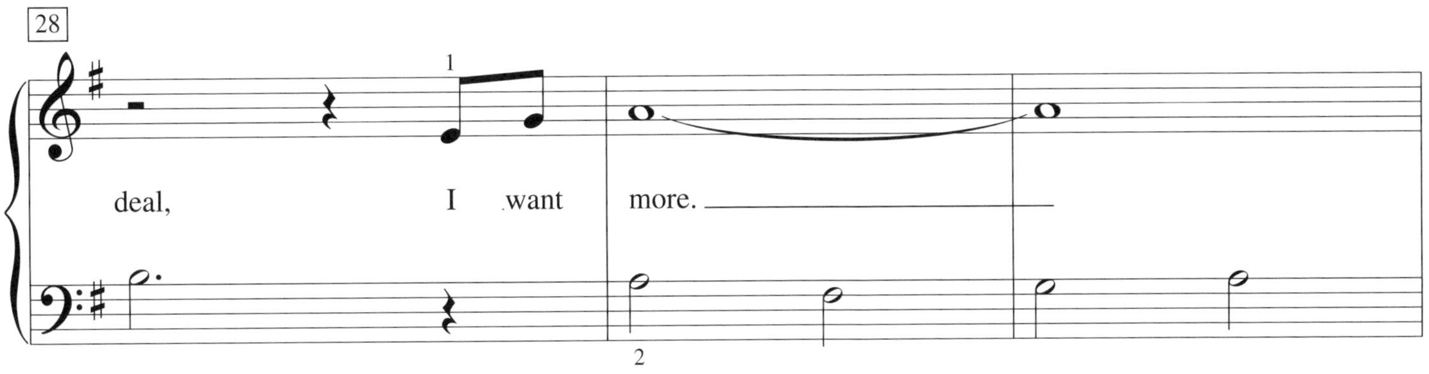
28
1
deal, I want more.
2

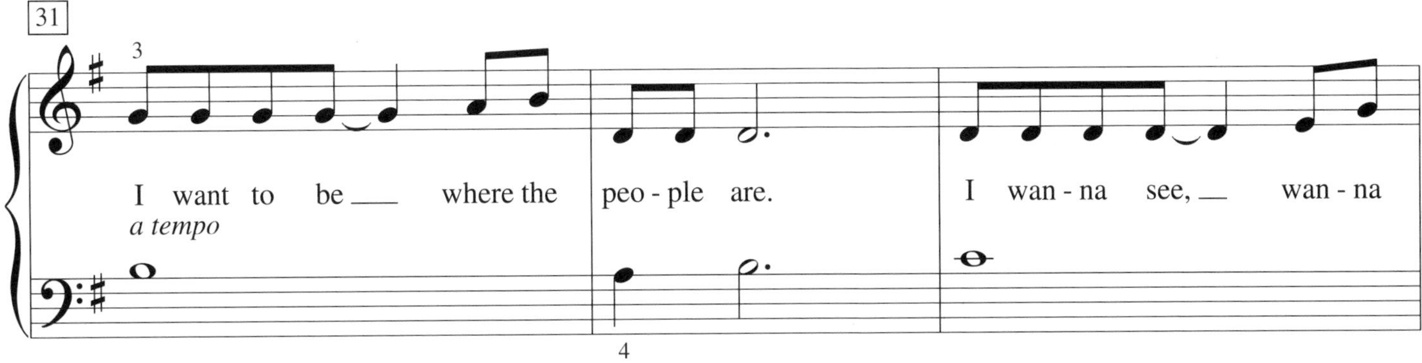
31
3
I want to be where the peo - ple are. I wan - na see, wan - na
a tempo
4

34
3
see 'em danc - in'. Walk - in' a - round on those, what - d' - ya call 'em? Oh...
3

28
31
a tempo
34

37
feet.
Flip - pin' your fins, ___ you don't
40
get too far.
Legs are re - qui - red for
jump - in', danc - in'.

43
Stroll - in' a - long ___ down the,
what's that word a - gain?
Street.

37
40
43

46
Up where they walk, up where they run, up where they stay all day in the

50
sun, wan-der-in' free, wish I could be part of that world.
L.H.
rit.
a tempo

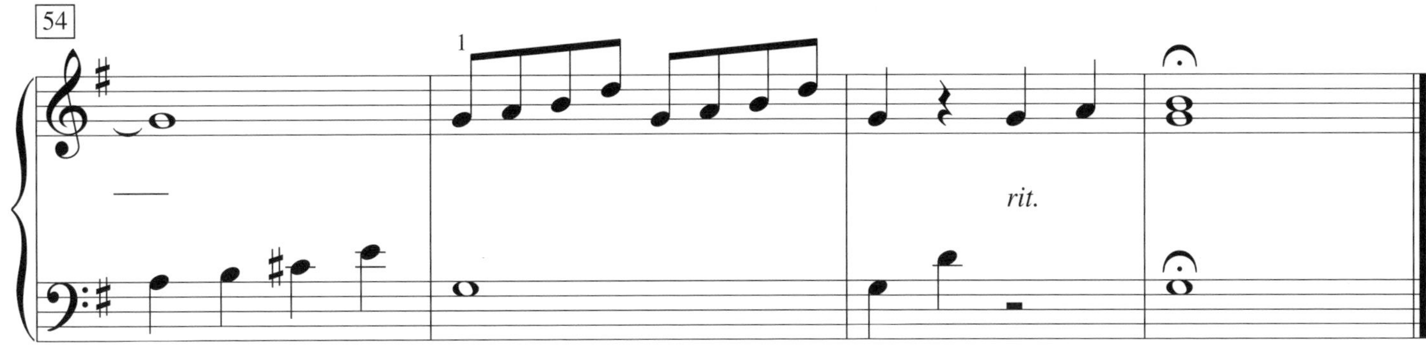
54
rit.

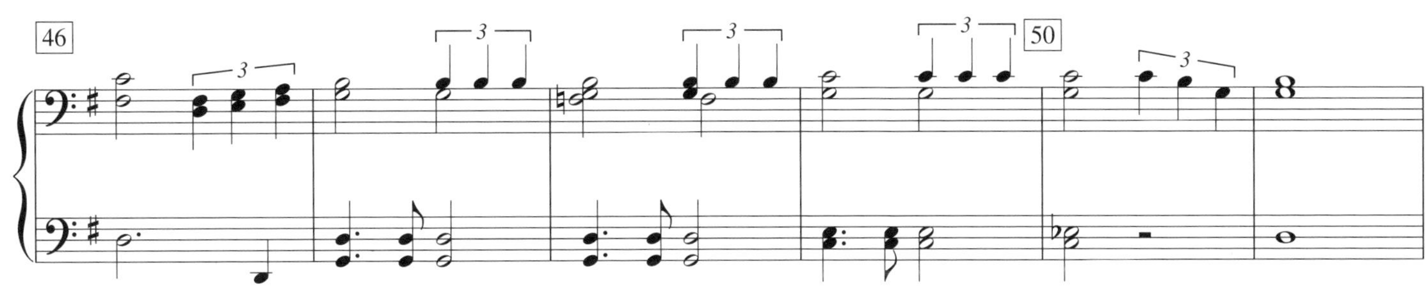
46
50

54
rit.
a tempo
rit.

Getting to Know You

from THE KING AND I

Use after Group III (page 18).

Lyrics by Oscar Hammerstein II
Music by Richard Rodgers
Arranged by Carolyn Miller

Accompaniment (Student plays one octave higher than written.)

14
2
5
4
2
You are pre - cise - ly my cup of tea! Get-ting to
L.H.
3
1

19
3
know you, get-ting to feel free and eas - y. When I am
3 3

23
3
3
with you, get-ting to know what to say. Have-n't you
3
4 3

14
3
19

23
3

27
no - ticed?
Sud-den-ly I'm bright and
breez - y
be - cause of
31
all the
beau-ti-ful and new
things I'm
learn-ing a-bout you
35
day
by
day.
27
31
35

The Surrey with the Fringe on Top

from OKLAHOMA!

Use after Group IV (page 24).

Lyrics by Oscar Hammerstein II
Music by Richard Rodgers
Arranged by Carolyn Miller

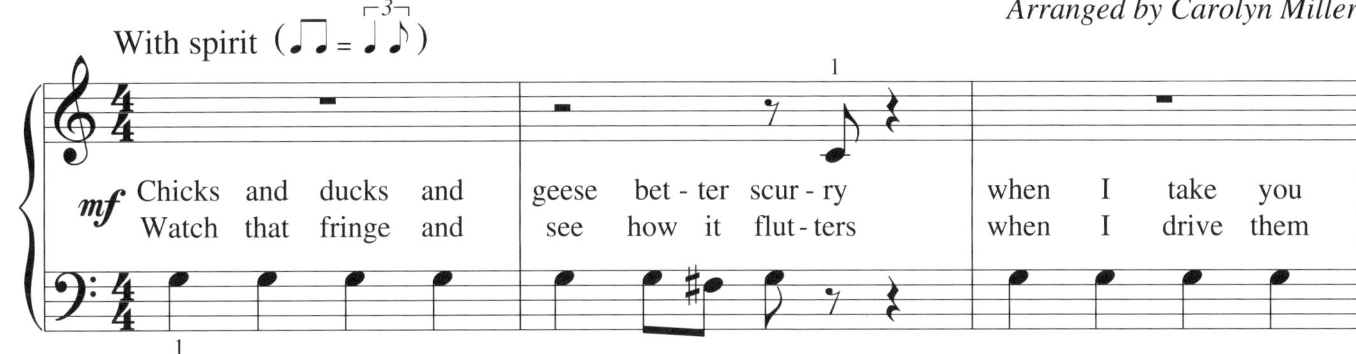

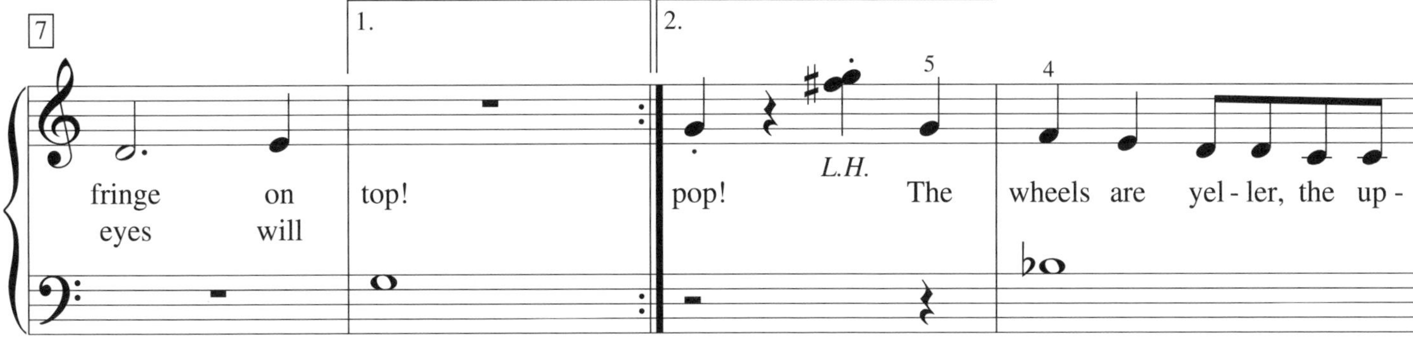

Accompaniment (Student plays one octave higher than written.)

11
hol - ster - y's brown, the
dash - board's gen - u - ine
leath - er, with

14
is - in - glass cur - tains y' can
roll right down, in
case there's a change in the

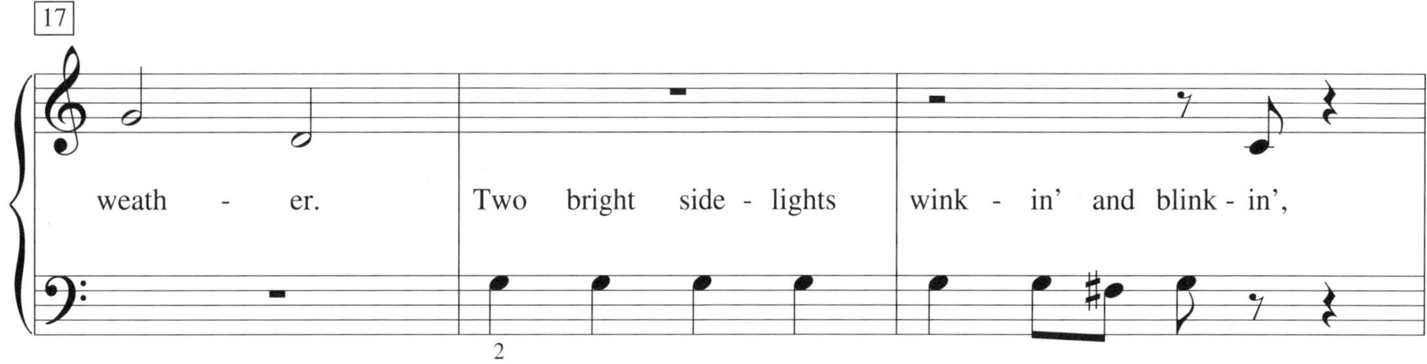
17
weath - er.
Two bright side - lights
wink - in' and blink - in',
2

11
14

17

20
ain't no fin - er
rig, I'm a think - in',
you c'n keep your

23
rig if you're think - in' 'at I'd
keer to
swap fer that

26
shin - y lit - tle sur - rey with the
fringe on the
top!

20
23

26

Swinging on a Star

Use after Group IV (page 24).

Words by Johnny Burke
Music by Jimmy Van Heusen

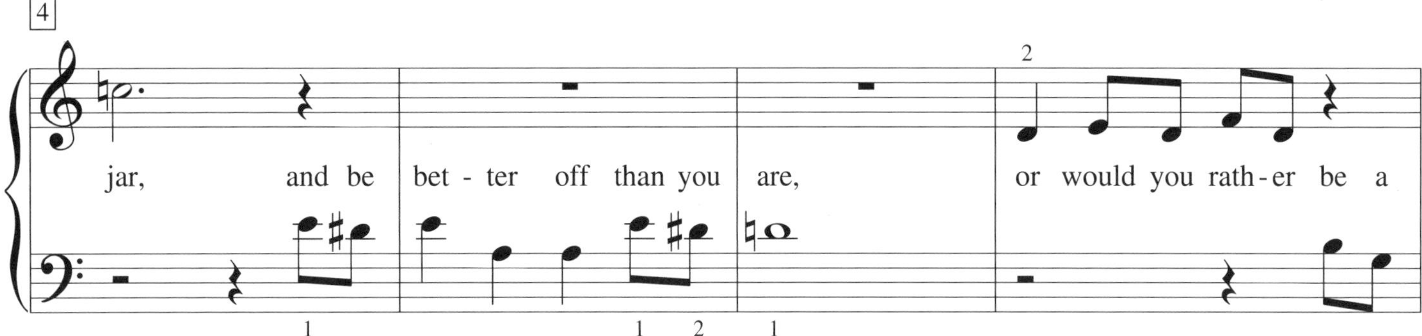

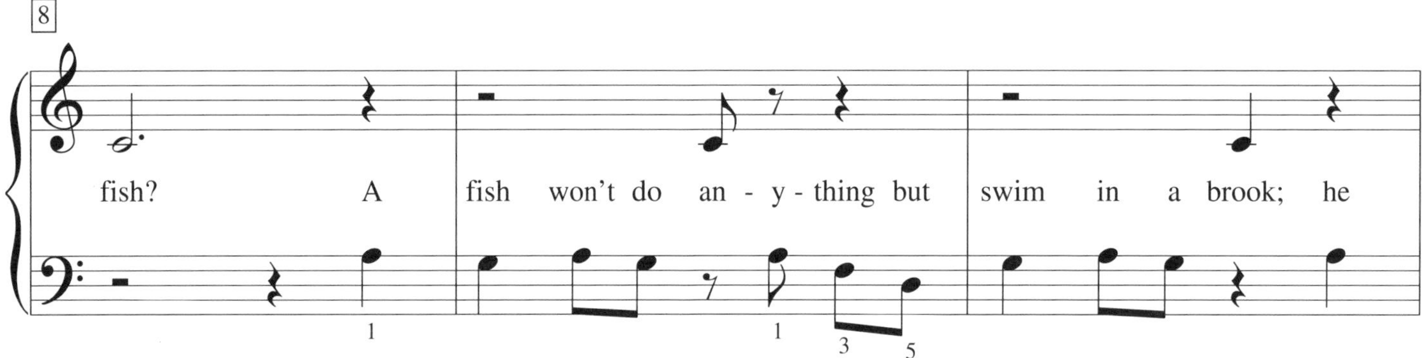

Accompaniment (Student plays one octave higher than written.)

11
4
3
5
can't write his name or read a book. To fool the peo - ple is his
1
14
3
5
3
3
on - ly thought, and though he's slip - per - y he still gets caught. But then if
3
17
that sort of life is what you wish, you may grow up to be a
1
11
14
17

20
fish. And all the mon - keys aren't in the zoo, ev - 'ry

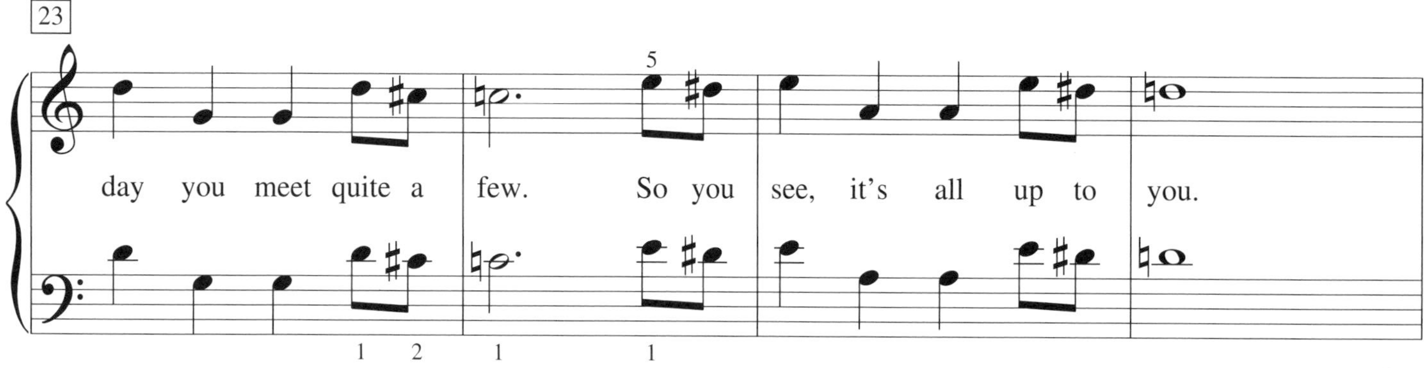
23
day you meet quite a few. So you see, it's all up to you.

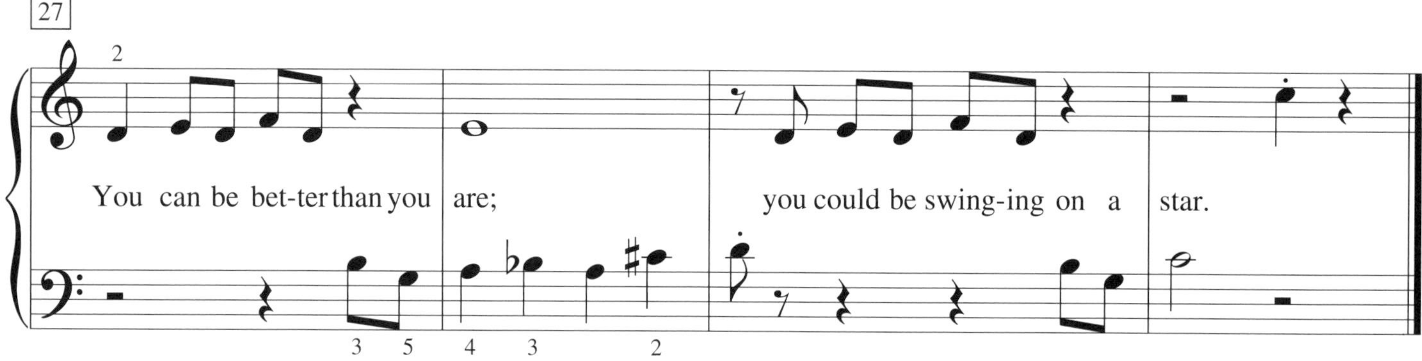
27
You can be bet-ter than you are; you could be swing-ing on a star.

20
23

27

The Bare Necessities

from Walt Disney's THE JUNGLE BOOK

Use after Group V (page 31).

Words and Music by
Terry Gilkyson
Arranged by Carolyn Miller

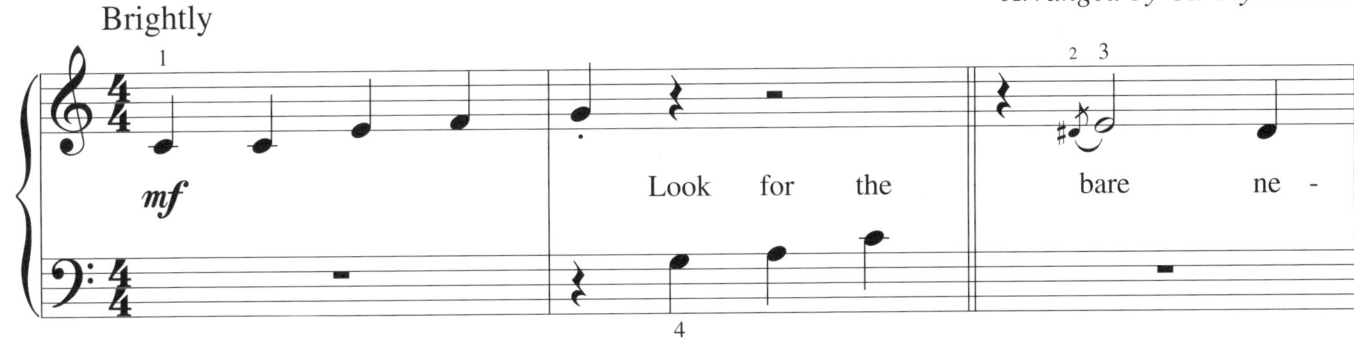

Accompaniment (Student plays one octave higher than written.)

12
ces - si - ties, oh, Moth - er Na - ture's rec - i - pes that bring the bare ne -

16
4
ces - si - ties of life. When - ev - er I wan - der,

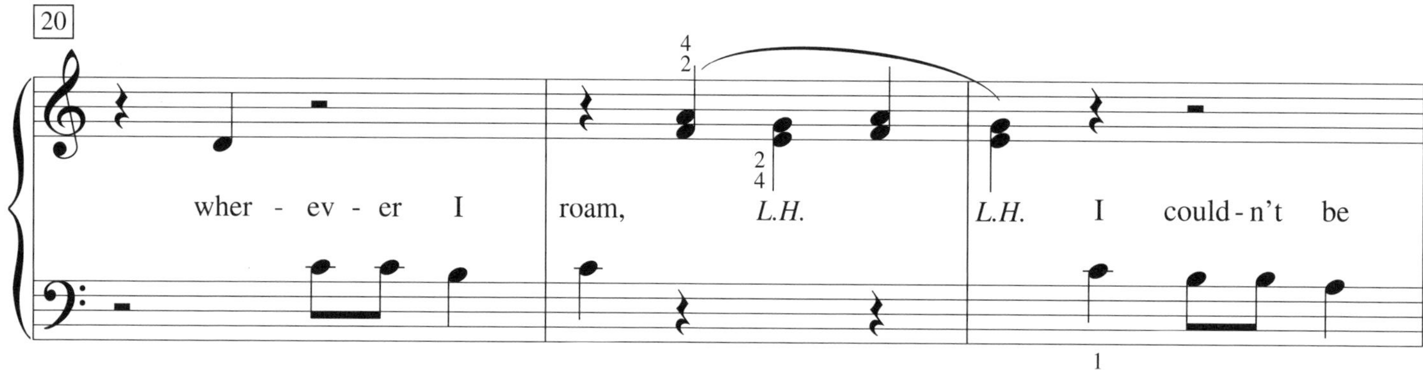
20
4
2
2
4
wher - ev - er I roam, L.H. L.H. I could - n't be
1

12
16

20

23
2
fond - er
of my big
home.
2
The bees are

27
5
buzz - in' in the
tree to make some
hon - ey just for
2
me. The bare ne -
5

31
ces - si - ties of
life will come to
4
2
you.
2
4
L.H.
L.H.

23
27
31

Do-Re-Mi

from THE SOUND OF MUSIC

Use after Group V (page 31).

Lyrics by Oscar Hammerstein II
Music by Richard Rodgers
Arranged by Carolyn Miller

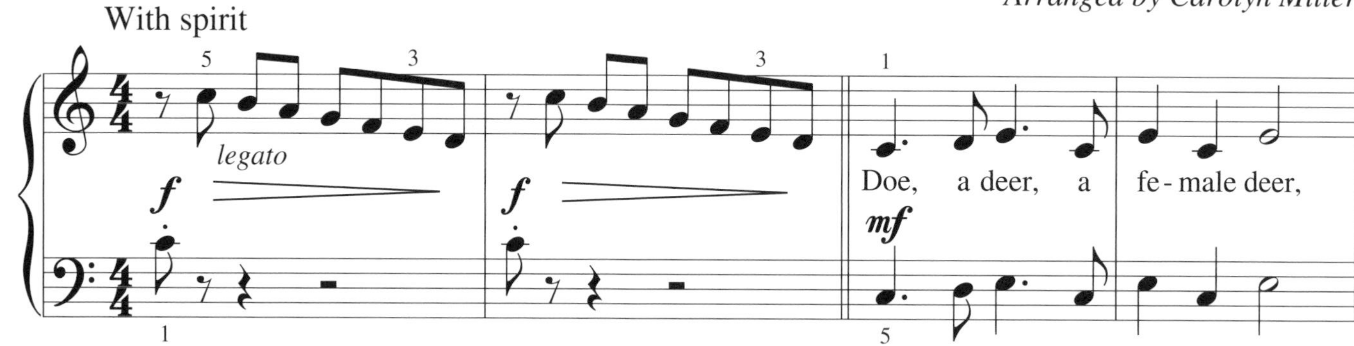

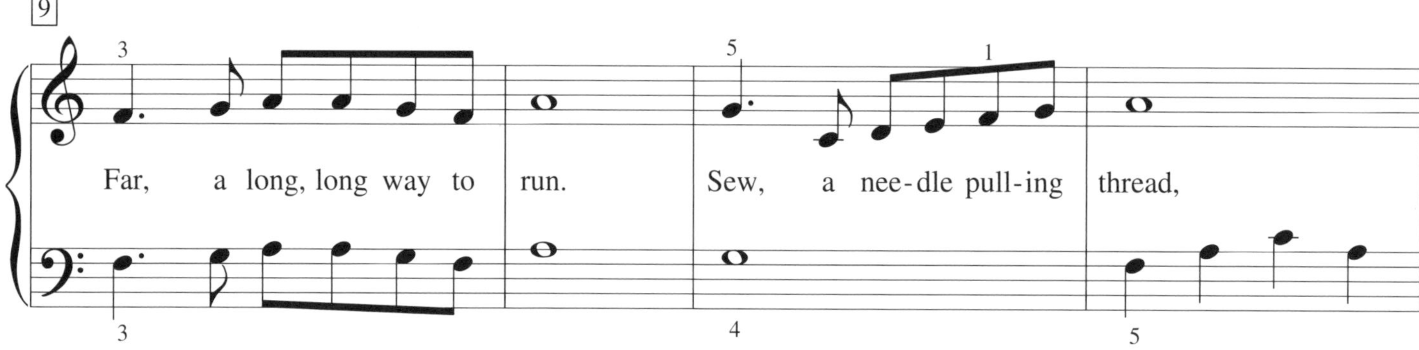

Accompaniment (Student plays one octave higher than written.)

13
La, a note to fol-low sew,
Tea, a drink with jam and bread that will
17
bring us back to do - oh - oh - oh!
f
21
13
17
21
mf

25
29
33
Do, re, mi, fa, sol, la, ti, do!
cresc.
f
25
29
33
cresc.
f